Living With the Tides

Written by Marilyn Woolley

Series Consultant: Linda Hoyt

WorldWise
Content-based Learning

Contents

1 | Where the land meets the sea

Find out more

Tides cause the water level at the edge of the sea to rise and fall each day. Most places on Earth have two low tides and two high tides every 24 hours. Find out about tides in your local area or in a place where you have visited. What times are the tides high and what times are they low?

It is early morning; the sun is up and you are on the sandy seashore. The tide is out and there is a wide stretch of sand in front of you. The sand is covered all over with lines and patterns of tracks. You wonder: What creatures made these marks? Why were these animals here? What were they doing? Where are they now?

Sandy seashores, rocky platforms and rock pools are found at the edge of the sea where the tide comes in. Places at the edge of the sea are made up of sand or mud that is constantly moved by winds, waves and tides. They are harsh places for plants and animals to live.

Yet plants and animals live in these places that at times are covered by salt water and at other times are exposed to the hot sun or strong winds. Which plants and animals survive in these different and changing tidal habitats? Why are tidal habitats now threatened? What can you do to help?

Tidal habitats

The tidal zone lies between the high- and low-tide lines on coastal habitats. As the tides move in and out at the edge of the seas they bring with them winds that cause ripples on the surface water called waves. Stronger winds and tides mean stronger waves.

Sandy beaches

Tides play an important role in beach habitats because they constantly change the depth of water in which waves come towards the coastline and strike the beach. If the waves are strong, sand is washed away from the shoreline as the tide moves out. Incoming tides can push the sand up higher, creating sand dunes. At first glance, these sandy beaches may not seem to have many animals at all. But most of the animals that live here are so small that they may not be noticed or they are hidden from view in their burrows.

Estuaries and mudflats

An estuary is a body of shallow water where a river meets the sea. Tides flow up an estuary twice a day and bring more salt water into it. The river brings freshwater and **sediment** such as sand, mud and small rocks as it flows out into the sea. The bottom of an estuary is often muddy.

Rock pools

Rock pools are found on rocky shelves. They are made from the **depressions** in the rocks and have sandy bottoms. Rocks break off from the sides of these pools and rest on the sand. Other rocks are washed in with the waves. Seawater stays in some rock pools after the tide has gone out.

Tides **submerge** or expose these parts of the coastal shoreline every six hours. The animals and plants that inhabit the tidal zone have to survive strong winds, shifting sediments, salt spray, and extreme heat and sun. They have developed interesting ways of doing this.

Chapter 2 | Plants in the tidal zone

The sand, salty air, water and strong winds at the seashore can be a harsh environment. But there are plants that grow along the shoreline and in the shallow seawater. Plants need sunlight, moisture and oxygen to survive.

Plants use the energy from the sun to make their own food. Often, the water near the shoreline is shallow and sunlight can reach the marine plants that grow there.

Seashore plants do not need much fresh water. They store moisture in their fat fleshy leaves. These thick leaves also protect them from the sun, and from the salt spray from the wind and the waves. These plants have their roots held in a firm place. Some marine plants attach to rocks so they are not washed away by pounding waves.

Find out more

At low tide, millions of tiny single-celled plants called **phytoplankton** live on the surface of the water and the moist sand. Phytoplankton make up the important beginning of the food chain for sea animals. Find out more about these food chains.

High tide

Low tide

Brown seaweeds such as kelp and red algae grow in deeper water that gets much less sunlight.

Seaweed

Seaweeds, sometimes called marine algae, are plants with no roots, stems, branches or leaves. They have fern-like fronds, and instead of having roots they have a **holdfast**, which acts like a suction cup and sticks to a firm surface.

Some seaweeds grow in the sandy bottom of the seabed and need to stay under water to survive. Others grow on rocks and shells.

Kelp is a type of seaweed. Kelp fronds have gas-filled bladders that help them float on the surface of the seawater where the sunlight is brightest.

Find out more

Seaweeds provide shelter and food for many sea animals, but how do seaweeds get their food? Find out more about how seaweeds get their food and oxygen.

Different seaweeds grow at different depths close to the low-tide line.

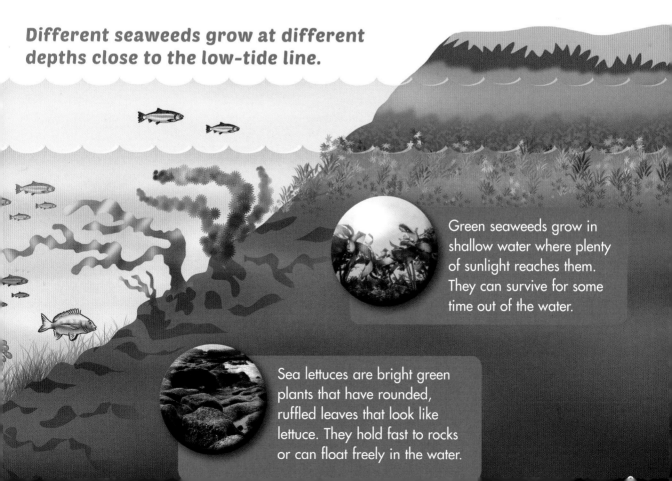

Green seaweeds grow in shallow water where plenty of sunlight reaches them. They can survive for some time out of the water.

Sea lettuces are bright green plants that have rounded, ruffled leaves that look like lettuce. They hold fast to rocks or can float freely in the water.

Seagrass

Seagrasses are flowering plants with roots, stems and leaves. They are able to live under the seawater. They cope with the salty conditions and grow well in the sandy or muddy **sediment** in calm shallow water. Their roots hold down the sediment and help prevent it from being washed away.

Mangroves

Seagrass

Estuary plants

As the tides move in and out of estuaries, lots of changes happen in the depth of the water, and plants living there need to cope with these changes. The amount of saltiness in the water changes, the temperature of the water changes and the changing depth of the water affects the amount of light that gets through to plants.

Mangrove plants can tolerate salt and flooding from incoming tides. They grow in soft mud and they put up special roots that poke above the mud. They take in oxygen through these roots and can filter the salt out of the water they take in through their roots.

Bulrushes and **sedges** have long underground stems and roots that creep sideways through the mud and keep the plants anchored there.

Bulrushes

Plants in estuaries get a lot of nutrients from the **brackish** water because bacteria in both the salt water and the freshwater breaks down plant and animal matter.

Animals in the tidal zone

Most animals living in tidal zone habitats rely on having some time each day under the water when the tide comes in, and some time out of the water when the tide goes out. When they are out of the water, these animals must be able to stop their bodies from overheating or drying out. Marine animals that live in tidal environments have body features and behaviours that allow them to survive in shallow water, on sandy and muddy shorelines and in rock pools.

Shallow tidal water animals

Herbivores

Dugongs, seahorses, and green sea turtles all feed on or shelter in the seagrass that grows on the ocean floor near the edge of the sea. These animals are herbivores and they need the seagrass that grows in the shallow water where there is plenty of sunlight.

A dugong has heavy bones so it can stay on the seafloor and eat seagrass. It is the only marine mammal that eats plants. It is known as a sea cow and can eat around 45 kilograms of seagrass each day.

Seahorses curl their tail around the stems of the seagrass to stay put as they feed on other sea creatures.

Green sea turtles eat seagrass and seaweed close to the shore. They use their rough beak, which has two rows of notches like a breadknife, to saw off chunks from the plant. When seagrass dies, it is washed up onto beaches and provides shelter for animals such as worms and sand hoppers.

Large predators

Large predators such as dolphins and some sharks swim in with the high tide to hunt for food in the shallow waters along coastlines and in estuaries at low tide. Bull sharks come into this shallow water to feed on seals, sea lions and small fish.

Some dolphins work together to herd and trap fish. They slap the surface of the water with their **flukes**, which make a splash of bubbles that startles the fish. They jump up into the air and the dolphins eat them. Large dolphins also eat sea lions and seals.

In estuaries, dolphins hit the muddy bottom with their flukes. This makes a ring of mud around the fish. The fish panic and leap up into the dolphins' mouths.

Some stingrays bury part of their bodies in the sandy ocean floor or in the mud at the bottom of estuaries. Stingrays flap their fins against the sand or the mud to uncover oyster and clam shells and then open them with their strong jaws and teeth plates.

Small predators

Terrapins are small predators that can survive in estuaries. When it rains, they raise their heads and drink the freshwater on the surface. Terrapins use their strong jaws to crush the shells of shrimp, clams, crabs, periwinkles and mussels.

In shallow estuary waters, **mangroves** provide homes or shelter for many smaller animals. Insects, spiders and snails live on the trunks of these trees. Crabs, shrimp, mussels and large numbers of small fish live in the water and mud around mangrove roots.

 Find out more

As the tide comes in, oysters draw in water, oxygen, plankton and algae through their gills into their mouths. When the tide goes out, they close their shells to protect themselves and they change the way they breathe. Find out about the life cycle of an oyster.

Animals in the sand or mudflats

Stretches of sand or mud are uncovered at low tide. Animals that feed in the sand flats and mudflats may die if they are exposed at low tide for long periods on very hot summer days. Some mud or sand dwellers are blind; others have eyes that rise above the sand or mud on long stalks. They behave in different ways to stay moist and to get protection from the sun.

Sand bubbler crabs live in burrows in the sand. At low tide they move through the surface layers of the sand. They take in sand to feed on tiny organic bits of decaying matter that live there. After feeding, they push the sand out of their mouthparts. The sand forms tiny bubbles on the surface of the beach.

Soldier crabs burrow into the mud or sand when they are feeding. As they do this, they pump water through their burrows and put oxygen into the **sediment**. When it is cool, crabs move across the sand and graze on tiny algae plants.

A mudskipper is a fish that can survive for a short time out of water. Mudskippers can walk over mudflats on their fins. They carry seawater in their gill pouches so that they can breathe oxygen from the seawater. They fill their mouthparts with seawater so they can catch and swallow worms, insect larvae and small shrimp.

Animals such as cockles and clams have shells that are joined. They move with the incoming waves up and down the beach to find food. When they are covered with water, they open their shells and filter food from the water. When the tide goes out, they close their shells and bury themselves in the waterlogged sand.

Rock pool animals

Rock pools are a permanent home for some sea creatures. At low tide, when the water moves out of rock pools, some animals such as mussels, oysters, scallops and barnacles close up their hard shells and stay put. They can hold their breath and stay moist inside their shells even when they are exposed to sun for long periods of time.

When the tide comes in, water flushes into the rock pools and brings with it oxygen, nutrients, and food. The animals open their shells to filter food from the incoming tide. At the same time, the water washes the animal waste away from these pools.

Some animals move around in the rock pools, while others stay put.

Staying put

Some animals attach themselves to one place in a rock pool. They have features that allow them to cling to the rocks so they are not washed away with the waves or eaten by other animals.

Abalones have a foot with a muscle that acts like a suction cup to cling to rocks. They scrape up loose pieces of seaweed with their zipper-like tongue.

Sea anemones have a sticky muscular foot that they use to hold on to rocks. They have venomous tentacles that they use to capture and paralyse fish, worms, crabs and shrimp.

Conesnails bury almost all their body in the sand and use venom from a tube on the top of their head to paralyse fish, worms and other snails.

Moving around

Many marine animals cannot survive out of the water for long periods of time. When the tide goes out, they need to move to deeper water. Other marine animals need to move to find food and shelter.

Sea slugs do not have a shell and must be covered by water to survive. They are found in deeper tidal pools. They eat sponges, anemones and barnacles. They take on the colour of the food they eat, which helps them avoid being seen.

Sea urchins move from spot to spot to eat seaweed, especially kelp and sea lettuce. Sea urchins can withstand a short period of time out of water. They can also jam themselves into holes in rocks and defend themselves with their sharp spines. A sea urchin hides by using its spikes to collect debris.

Limpets and sea snails move around slowly in tidal pools, grazing on algae. They are less active when exposed to air during low tide; they also eat algae on the rock surface.

Sea stars crawl into the water to eat molluscs and sea lettuce. Tiny crabs can live among the sea star's tube feet, eating scraps of dead marine animals.

A tidal zone food web

1 Tiny plants are eaten by tiny animals and mussels
2 Mussels are eaten by sea stars
3 Sea stars are eaten by seagulls
4 Seagrass is eaten by manatees and green sea turtles
5 Limpets are eaten by crabs
6 Fish are eaten by seagulls
7 Sea snails are eaten by fish
8 Seaweed is eaten by sea snails and limpets
9 Worms and crabs are eaten by birds
10 Crabs are eaten by seals

4 | Visitors

Tidal environments are important to animals that visit them. Animals visit tidal environments to hunt for food. Sandy beaches provide places for female animals to lay their eggs. In turn, these eggs or the animals that hatch from them become food for visiting animals.

Silver gulls, terns and birds of prey such as sea eagles and kites are regular visitors to sandy beaches. Birds that visit the shoreline to feed have particular behaviours and features. Most species of wading birds have long legs and long toes to stand in shallow water or walk on mud or wet sand without sinking. Their beaks are different shapes and lengths so some can dig deeper than others, and groups of wading birds can take different types of food from the same place.

On pebbly coastal beaches, rock sandpipers use their beaks to flick over small stones, pick off shrimp, or turn over shells and eat the animals inside.

Large groups of oystercatchers spread across the mudflats feeding on worms, crabs and mussels. They use their flat, heavy bills to pry open crab shells and smash mussel shells.

Herons have very long toes that keep them from sinking too far into the mud. They pace slowly to stalk their prey and stab it with their sharp, pointed beaks.

Did you know?

Penguins cannot fly. They wait until the tide comes in and they dive off the rocks or sand into the water and swim away.

Using coastal places to nest or raise young

Some animals come to the same coastlines each year to breed and raise their young. They can easily find plenty of food in the nearby sea. Some animals make nests on island shores and others nest on rocky coastal cliffs.

Find out more

Make a list of reptiles that build their nests on sandy banks in estuaries.

Birds
Many species of birds make nests in coastal places. Tufted puffins nest in colonies on coastal rocky cliffs. Sooty terns come ashore from the open ocean only to nest in salt marshes and on beaches. Different types of penguins come ashore to make nests and raise chicks.

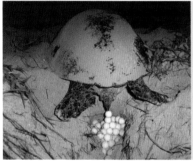

Nesting reptiles
Sea turtles come ashore to make a nest and lay their eggs on the same sandy slopes where they had been hatched. Their young have to find their own way back to the shoreline and catch the tides to get out to sea where many become food for herons.

Mammals
Sea lions come ashore to breed. They shelter with their young in the shallow waters of bays and estuaries. Sea lions form large groups on rocky and sandy beaches when they are breeding and giving birth. Young sea lions shelter in groups in shallow water while their mothers go out to sea to feed.

Roebuck Bay: A visitor's

Find out more

Roebuck Bay was designated a Ramsar Wetland of International Importance in June 1990. Find out about other tidal Ramsar wetlands in Australia.

Each year, over 300,000 shorebirds visit Roebuck Bay on the north coast of Western Australia. This estuary is one of the most important migration stopovers for shorebirds in Australia and the world.

Shorebirds such as plovers, sandpipers and godwits nest and breed in northern China and Siberia during summer in the northern hemisphere. At the end of summer, they travel from Siberia and China, and arrive in Roebuck Bay in September or October.

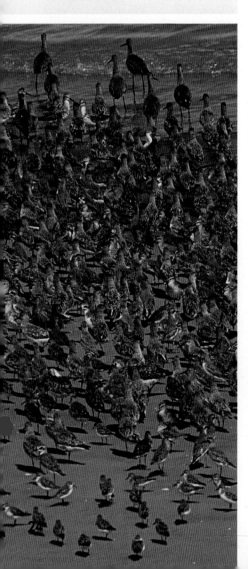

When the birds arrive, they are tired and hungry. They find food on the mudflats and sandy beaches to build up their body fat. They feast on 300–500 different species of invertebrates such as crabs, snails, shellfish and worms. They also moult and then grow new feathers before leaving Roebuck Bay in late March to early May. When they leave, they return to the northern hemisphere to nest and breed.

Siberia

CHINA

Pacific Ocean

Roebuck Bay ○

AUSTRALIA

The shaded area shows where migratory shorebirds travel.

Other animals use this estuary, too. Juvenile prawns and mud crab larvae visit the estuary's mangroves to feed and grow before moving out to the open sea.

Dugongs, green sea turtles and loggerhead turtles visit the estuary's large seagrass beds each year to find food.

5 | Threats

Tidal environments are fragile places that can be easily disturbed by the forces of nature or by the activities of people. Strong winds, king tides, waves and heavy rainfall can wash away coastal plant and animal habitats. Urban development in coastal environments can create pollution that affects tidal areas. These things threaten the survival of animals and plants that rely on tidal environments.

Threats from nature

The **ecosystems** around the tidal zone are harsh, fragile places that are easily harmed by nature.

Strong storms

Strong winds in severe storms cause large waves to crash onto the shore and churn up or wash away sand, animals and plants. High tides and extremely heavy rainfall can also damage coastal ecosystems.

Earthquakes

Sometimes an earthquake causes a huge wall of water called a **tsunami** to rush towards the shoreline. The first sign of a tsunami is when the tide pulls the water right back from the shoreline, sucking up many seashore plants, animals and sand. After that, a great wall of water rushes back to the shoreline in the form of a tidal wave and floods the land way beyond the shoreline. This causes great damage and afterward, many seashore plants and animals do not return to their homes so there is less food for the animals that remain. This damage to the shoreline can also affect migrating birds because they must look elsewhere for food and shelter.

Threats from people

At any time, and in any weather, tidal habitats are very fragile. But people's activities can be harmful and long lasting. The balance and interconnectedness of the plants and animals can easily be destroyed so that living things may suffer or even die.

Changing coastlines

In some coastal places, mudflats and **mangrove** areas are drained to make way for houses, factories, crops or power stations. All sorts of chemicals, fertilisers, and waste pollution flow from these places into the tidal ecosystem. As this happens, the makeup of the water is changed and then algae take over, smothering other plants and small animals.

Contamination

There is always the risk of contamination from oil spills at sea. Oil in the water is damaging to birds, as it can clog up their feathers or they can swallow it when they are preening.

Also, some oil refineries and power stations release warm water into rivers, which heats up the cold river water. Warm water has less oxygen than cold water and marine animals and plants can suffer and die in warm water.

Climate change

Our planet is getting warmer because our climate is rapidly changing. The ocean acts like a sponge and soaks up and holds heat. Warm air and warmer ocean temperatures mean that ice caps and ice sheets are melting faster. As ice melts, sea levels rise. The tides and waves get higher and some coastal places flood. Greater amounts of warmer water will change the conditions in coastal habitats. Many sea plants and animals may not adjust to these new conditions and will die.

Conclusion

We are fortunate that there are still stretches of coastline that have not been built on or polluted. This is frequently the achievement of groups of people who work hard to protect these areas as nature reserves.

Because many of the plants and animals living in tidal zones are small, they are sometimes not noticed when people visit these areas. During our visits to these fragile places, we need to be very careful.

Things to remember

✔ Leave rocks the way you find them. The creatures living under the rocks may die if the rocks are moved.

✔ Leave living things where you find them. If you move them from one spot to another, they may die.

✔ Be careful not to crush animals and plants when you're walking.

✔ Wear clean shoes. Don't bring dirt from other places on your shoes or feet. This can harm animals and plants.

✔ Don't dig. You might smother animals with sand from the pile you make.

Glossary

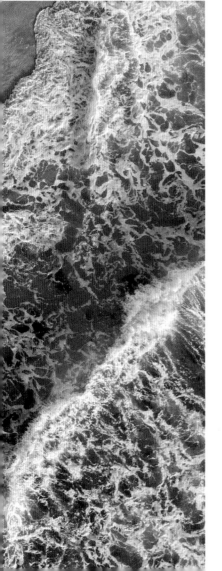

brackish water that is slightly salty

bulrushes tall, reedy water plants

depressions places on a surface that are lower than the surrounding area

ecosystem everything in a particular environment including living and nonliving things

fluke one of the two triangular parts on a dolphin's tail

holdfast the root-like part of a water plant that attaches the plant to a surface

mangrove a plant that grows in coastal areas, usually with roots that grow above ground

migratory moving from one place to another to find food or look after young

phytoplankton tiny, single-celled plants that live on the surface of the water

sedge a water plant similar to grass but with a solid stem

sediment the material that settles at the bottom of a body of water, such as sand and stones

submerge to put underwater

terrapin a type of turtle that lives in fresh or slightly salty water

tsunami a massive sea wave that forms due to an earthquake underneath the ocean

Index